Philosophy of Residential and Commercial Real Estate
Exploring the Intersection of Philosophy, People, Property, Purpose and Spaces

By Willem Tait

Published by WRT Publishing

WRT
PUBLISHING

Copyright © 2024 by Willem Tait - All rights reserved.

Copyright Warning: No part of this publication may be reproduced, distributed, or transmitted in any form or by any means, including photocopying, recording, or other electronic or mechanical methods, without the prior written permission of the author, except in the case of brief quotations embodied in reviews and certain other noncommercial uses permitted by copyright law.

For permission requests, contact the author at:
willemtait@outlook.com

Disclaimer: This eBook is for educational and informational purposes only. The author is not liable for any damages or losses arising from the use or misuse of the content.

Cover Design: Time Brands
Published by WRT Publishing

First Edition (2024)
Revised Edition (2025)
This edition includes updated formatting, new front and back matter, and added glossaries for philosophy and real estate. It reflects the continued refinement of the author's work on the philosophy behind residential and commercial real estate.

KDP Amazon ISBN Print Paperback: 9798303327184
KDP Amazon ISBN print Hardcover: 9798303329836
Library Print ISBN: 978-0-6398578-6-2
Library eBook ISBN: 978-0-6398578-7-9

Why This Book and Why Now

Why should you read a book on real estate philosophy? Because it reveals the deeper forces that shape value, behavior, and opportunity.

For investors, professionals, and thinkers alike, this book offers a simple truth: **the more deeply you understand real estate, the more you can profit from it.**

Those who understand these forces gain a lasting advantage in every negotiation and decision.

Here you will discover how awareness in real estate creates opportunity, how ethics and design influence demand, and how clarity of thought translates into smarter, more sustainable success.

Let the journey begin.

Table of Contents

Why This Book and Why Now 3
Table of Contents 4
Introduction 8
CHAPTER 1: Introduction to Philosophy and Real Estate 11
    How philosophy shapes our understanding of property and space 11
    Conclusion: Value, Ownership, Ethics, Connection 15
CHAPTER 2: Value and Worth (Axiology) 18
    Exploring the philosophical roots of value in residential and commercial property. 18
    Conclusion: Intrinsic and Extrinsic Worth 23
CHAPTER 3: Ownership and Rights (Ontology) 26
    The nature of ownership: philosophical and practical dimensions. 26
    Conclusion: Entitlement, Stewardship, Legality ... 30
CHAPTER 4: Emotional Connection to Real Estate (Entomology) 33
    Exploring the emotional bonds that connect us to the spaces we own and use. 33
    Conclusion: Pride, Identity, Connection, Memories. 37
CHAPTER 5: Politics and Governance (Polity) 40
    The philosophical role of governance in shaping real estate landscapes. 40

Conclusion: Zoning, Rules, Urban Planning, Taxation 45

CHAPTER 6: Spatial and Relational Dynamics (Typology) 47

Philosophical insights into the types and relationships of spaces. 47

Conclusion: Interaction, Connect, Physical, Impact, Dynamics 52

CHAPTER 7: Environmental Considerations (Ecology) 54

The philosophy of sustainability in real estate. 54

Conclusion: Environment, Ethics, Responsibility, Conservation..59

CHAPTER 8: Cultural and Social Constructs (Sociology) 61

The cultural philosophy behind real estate trends and societal norms...61

Conclusion: Trends, Community, Cohesion, Gentrification..66

CHAPTER 9: Habitation and Space (Anthropology) 68

Philosophical reflections on human habitation and the need for shelter...68

Conclusion: Shelter, Design, Identity, Evolution, Belonging. 73

CHAPTER 10: Transformative Impacts and Trends (Technology) 75

The philosophy of innovation in reshaping real estate. 75

Conclusion: Progress, Adaptation, Transformation, Connection..80

CHAPTER 11: Market Forces (Economy) 82
    Philosophical underpinnings of market forces in real estate. 82
    Conclusion: Scarcity, Opportunity, Supply, Demand, Fairness, Trends. 87

CHAPTER 12: Spatial Identity, Place, and Self (Topology) 89
    The philosophy of place and its impact on identity. 89
    Conclusion: Geography, Community, Self, Personal, Communal, Feelings, Design, Structure. 94

CHAPTER 13: Market Interconnectivity and Systems (Globality) 96
    The philosophical implications of global real estate connections. 96
        Conclusion and Call to Action 101

CHAPTER 14: Housing Philosophy Societal Reflections 103
    Philosophical reflections on housing as a societal cornerstone. 103
    Conclusion: Dignity, Equality, Exclusion, Inclusion, Progress 108

CHAPTER 15: Summation - Real Estate, Philosophy, and the Path Ahead 110
    Reflecting on the philosophical journey of real estate. 110
    Conclusion: Property, People, Ideas, Spaces 114

Glossary 117
Bonus Section: Case Studies and Reflections 123
Updated List of Books to Date 129
Acknowledgement 133
Social Profiles 135

Mentorship, Coaching, Consulting and Public Speaking 137
Author Bio 139
Upcoming Projects 142
We Value Your Feedback! 143
    Portfolio of Books by Willem Tait 148

Introduction

Real estate is everywhere. It's in the homes we live in, the offices we work in, and the places we gather to shop, dine, and connect. But beyond the bricks and mortar, beyond the financial transactions, there's a deeper story, a philosophical one. What if I told you that real estate is more than property or investments?

It's a reflection of who we are, how we live, and what we value as a society. This book invites you to uncover that story, exploring the profound connection between people, spaces, and ideas.

At first glance, real estate might seem like a practical, straightforward field, buying, selling, building, and investing. But dig deeper, and you'll find that it's intertwined with philosophy in ways that shape our identity, influence our communities, and define our aspirations.

Whether it's a family searching for their dream home or a company establishing its global headquarters, real estate reflects human values at every level.

This book is for everyone: the curious philosopher, the seasoned property professional, and anyone in between. It's for those who want to understand not just the mechanics of real estate but its meaning. Together, we'll explore questions that go beyond price tags and floor plans. What makes a house a home? How do commercial spaces influence culture and community? What role does governance play in shaping the places we inhabit?

In the chapters ahead, we'll dive into concepts like value, ownership, sustainability, and connection, blending philosophical insights with real-world examples from both residential and commercial real estate.

From zoning laws to emotional ties, from urban planning to global markets, this book bridges the abstract and the tangible, showing how real estate is both a product and a driver of human thought and behavior.

As you read, I encourage you to think about your own relationship with real estate. Perhaps it's a family home that holds cherished memories or a business property that's been a cornerstone of your success.

Maybe it's a dream of ownership, a question of belonging, or simply a curiosity about the spaces that surround us. Whatever your perspective, this book will help you see real estate through a new lens, one that combines logic with emotion, practicality with philosophy.

Real estate is not just about property, it's about people. It's about the spaces we build, the lives we live within them, and the connections they create. By the time you finish this book, you'll have a deeper understanding of how these elements intertwine, shaping not only markets but the human experience itself.

Let's dive in. I promise you, you'll never look at real estate the same way again.

CHAPTER 1: Introduction to Philosophy and Real Estate

How philosophy shapes our understanding of property and space

What is philosophy? At its core, philosophy is the study of fundamental questions about existence, values, and meaning. Philosophy might not be the first thing that comes to mind when we think about real estate, but perhaps it should be. At its heart, real estate isn't just about transactions, locations, or investments, it's about people, their values, and the spaces that shape their lives.

Philosophy provides us with the tools to ask deeper questions about what these spaces mean and how they affect our sense of identity, belonging, and purpose.

Take, for example, a family buying their first home. For them, it's not just a property; it's the foundation of their future, a canvas for their dreams. The choice of the neighborhood reflects their values, whether they prioritize proximity to schools, community safety, or a vibrant social atmosphere.

Real estate isn't just a financial decision; it's an ethical and emotional one, rooted in how they see their lives unfolding.

Now consider the commercial realm, like a bustling retail complex or a towering office building. These spaces aren't just structures for commerce, they're hubs of activity that define how businesses operate and how people interact. A retail developer must balance financial viability with creating a space that feels inviting and serves the needs of the community. Here, philosophy intersects with practicality, as developers consider questions about purpose, connectivity, and sustainability.

Ownership is another area where philosophy plays a key role. What does it mean to truly own something?

In residential real estate, homeownership is often seen as a milestone of independence and security, but it also comes with responsibility, maintaining the property, contributing to the community, and respecting the environment. In commercial real estate, ownership often has a broader impact. A landlord managing an office building isn't just providing space; they're shaping the environment where ideas flourish and businesses grow.

Ethics is an unavoidable thread in both residential and commercial real estate.

Imagine a landlord deciding on rental terms for tenants. Do they prioritize profit at all costs, or do they consider affordability and fairness? Similarly, in commercial settings, how do developers approach urban planning? Are they driven purely by financial gain, or do they seek to contribute to a city's long-term sustainability and livability? These decisions reflect philosophical beliefs about what is right, just, and beneficial for society.

Spaces themselves carry a philosophical weight.

A home can represent comfort and stability, while an office might symbolize ambition and collaboration. Yet both residential and commercial spaces can also be exclusionary, reinforcing divides between those who have access to opportunity and those who do not. Recognizing this, real estate becomes more than just a business, it becomes a platform for addressing societal values and shaping communities.

Even the concept of value ties deeply to philosophy.

In residential real estate, a house may be valued for its size, location, or design, but its true worth often lies in the memories and connections it fosters. In commercial real estate, value can be calculated through income streams and market performance, but what about the less tangible value, how a space energizes its occupants or enhances a community?

Philosophical inquiry helps us look beyond the surface to understand the essence of value in real estate.

As we move through this book, these ideas will guide us, offering a lens to see real estate as more than a market or industry. By blending philosophy with the practical realities of property, we can better understand how the spaces we create and inhabit influence us, and how we, in turn, shape those spaces. Real estate is not just a transaction; it's a reflection of who we are and what we value.

Conclusion: Value, Ownership, Ethics, Connection

This chapter has set the stage for a deeper exploration of the philosophy of residential and commercial real estate.

Real estate is more than property transactions or architectural designs; it is a reflection of human values, aspirations, and connections. The spaces we inhabit influence how we live, work, and interact, shaping our sense of belonging and identity. By bridging the abstract with the tangible, we've begun to uncover the deeper meaning behind the places we call our own.

The questions raised here, about value, ownership, ethics, and connection, serve as a foundation for understanding real estate beyond its practical functions.

These concepts guide the way we think about property, whether as a family home, an investment, or a business opportunity. They also prompt us to consider the broader implications of how our choices impact communities, environments, and even future generations.

Next, we dive into the concept of value itself in Chapter 2 called Value and Worth, Axiology. Here, we will explore the philosophical roots of worth in real estate, from the intrinsic emotional ties that shape our connection to a family home to the extrinsic financial calculations that drive commercial investments. By understanding value in its many dimensions, we can uncover how it influences our decisions and the spaces we create. Let this journey deepen your perspective on real estate as more than property, it's a reflection of the values we hold.

READERS NOTES

CHAPTER 2: Value and Worth (Axiology)

Exploring the philosophical roots of value in residential and commercial property.

What is Axiology? Axiology is the branch of philosophy that studies values, including their nature, significance, and impact on our decisions. When we think about the value of real estate, the first thing that comes to mind is often the price tag, a number assigned to a property based on its location, size, and demand. But value is far more complex than a financial figure.

It carries layers of meaning that go beyond economics, delving into the emotional, societal, and even philosophical realms. What gives a property its worth? Is it intrinsic, something inherent to the property itself, or extrinsic, shaped by external factors like market trends and community perceptions?

In residential real estate, value often begins with the emotional connection people form with their homes.

A modest house can hold immense worth because it's where a family gathers, where children grow up, or where someone finally achieves the dream of homeownership. The walls of a home may be made of brick or wood, but its real value lies in the memories it shelters and the sense of security it provides.

These intrinsic elements, deeply personal and tied to human experience, make the value of a home something that goes beyond simple market calculations.

On the commercial side, value takes on a different yet equally multifaceted meaning. A bustling shopping center or a sleek office building may be appraised for its income potential or location, but its worth also lies in how it serves the people who use it. A retail space, for example, could be the lifeblood of a small business, representing opportunity and growth. An office building, meanwhile, might symbolize innovation and collaboration, housing the aspirations of countless employees and entrepreneurs.

These spaces are not just assets, they're environments that reflect the values of the people who occupy them.

Intrinsic and extrinsic value often intersect in ways that are hard to separate. Consider a home in a desirable neighborhood. Its intrinsic worth might come from its charm, layout, or design, but its extrinsic value is tied to the quality of the schools nearby, the safety of the streets, or the vibrancy of the community. In commercial real estate, a property's intrinsic qualities, like a well-designed floor plan or state-of-the-art facilities, might complement its extrinsic appeal, such as being located in a booming economic hub.

Together, these layers of value create a more complete picture of a property's worth.

Societal perceptions play a powerful role in shaping real estate value, whether residential or commercial. A neighborhood's reputation can elevate or diminish a home's worth, even if the house itself remains unchanged. Similarly, a commercial property in a gentrifying area may see its extrinsic value skyrocket, driven by changing societal attitudes and economic shifts.

Perceptions reveal how value in real estate is as much about societal dynamics as it is about the physical property itself.

Philosophy invites us to look deeper into these dynamics. It asks us to consider not just what we value but why we value it. For example, is a property's worth tied solely to its ability to generate income or enhance social standing? Or does its value also lie in how it contributes to human well-being, fosters community, or preserves history? These questions force us to rethink the way we define worth, particularly in real estate, where decisions often ripple out to affect entire communities.

Value systems guide every decision in real estate, from how properties are marketed to how they are developed and maintained.

In residential markets, developers might cater to luxury buyers, prioritizing exclusivity and status, while affordable housing projects emphasize equity and accessibility. In commercial markets, some developers may focus on profit maximization, while others take a longer-term view, prioritizing sustainability and community integration. These choices reflect underlying philosophies about what we collectively value as a society.

At its core, real estate value is about perception.

A homebuyer sees a dream fulfilled; an investor sees potential returns. A tenant sees a space to thrive; a developer sees a canvas for ambition. These perceptions, shaped by personal, social, and economic factors, weave together to create a complex tapestry of worth. And through this lens, real estate becomes more than a market, it becomes a mirror, reflecting the values of the people and societies it serves.

Conclusion: Intrinsic and Extrinsic Worth

This chapter has explored the many dimensions of value in real estate, bridging philosophy with practical realities. Whether it's the emotional significance of a family home or the economic potential of a commercial property, worth is always more than it seems.

Consider, for example, a hospital. It is a place of care where lives are saved, families gather in times of hope or healing, and new life begins.

Simultaneously, it is a place of work, generating income for its staff and landlords, with tenants like medical practitioners and pharmacies contributing to its commercial value. The hospital embodies both intrinsic and extrinsic worth, serving as a powerful reminder of how real estate reflects human values at every level. As we move forward, consider how your own values influence your decisions about real estate, whether you're buying, selling, developing, or simply dreaming.

With this understanding of worth as our foundation, we now turn to the concept of ownership.

In chapter 3 we will explore what it truly means to own property, delving into the philosophical interpretations of rights, entitlement, and stewardship, as well as the legal frameworks that shape real estate decisions.

Let's delve into the concept of ownership and its role in uncovering the deeper connections between property and human values.

READERS NOTES

CHAPTER 3: Ownership and Rights (Ontology)

The nature of ownership: philosophical and practical dimensions.

What is ontology? At its core, ontology is the branch of philosophy that deals with the nature of being, what exists, why it exists, and how we understand its existence. In real estate, this idea takes on a practical dimension as we explore what it means to "own" something. Ownership, after all, is not just a legal construct; it's a deeply human concept tied to identity, security, and responsibility.

To own property is to hold more than just a deed or title. It is to claim a space in the world, to say, "This is mine." For a homeowner, that might mean a place to build memories, raise a family, and feel safe. The sense of entitlement that comes with ownership is not merely about possession but about the right to shape a space according to one's needs and desires. Yet, ownership is also about stewardship. A home must be maintained, cared for, and preserved for future generations.

Philosophically, this interplay between entitlement and responsibility is central to the concept of ownership.

In the commercial real estate world, ownership operates on a broader scale but carries similar philosophical weight. Think of a business owner purchasing a retail space or an office building. Here, ownership is not just about personal use but about creating opportunities for others. The landlord or property owner takes on the role of a steward, ensuring that the property serves its purpose for tenants and contributes to the surrounding community. Yet, this stewardship is often balanced, or conflicted, with financial goals.

The question arises: to what extent is ownership a privilege, and to what extent is it an obligation?

Legal frameworks play a critical role in defining ownership, but they are only part of the story. Laws may outline who has the right to occupy, sell, or lease property, but the philosophical underpinnings of these rights delve deeper. In residential real estate, the right to ownership is often tied to ideas of autonomy and freedom. Owning a home signifies independence, a sense of achievement, and even a kind of self-determination. At the same time, it raises ethical questions:

Is it fair that some people can own vast amounts of property while others struggle for a roof over their heads?

In commercial settings, legal rights can become even more complex. A commercial landlord may have the legal right to evict a struggling tenant for nonpayment, but what about their ethical responsibilities? Does stewardship extend to ensuring the tenant has a fair chance to succeed, or is the relationship purely transactional? These scenarios highlight the tension between legal rights and moral obligations, a recurring theme in the philosophy of ownership.

Philosophy also asks us to consider what it means to own something that we didn't create.

Land, for example, existed long before anyone laid claim to it. Does ownership imply an inherent right to exploit that land as we see fit, or does it come with a duty to preserve and respect it? For residential property owners, this might mean maintaining their home in a way that respects their neighbors and the broader community. For commercial property owners, it could mean developing spaces responsibly, considering environmental impacts and the well-being of those who use the property.

Stewardship is a thread that runs through all forms of ownership.

A family that owns a home is entrusted not only with the care of that property but also with its place within the community. Their actions, whether planting a garden or hosting a neighborhood event, reflect a form of stewardship that extends beyond the property line. Similarly, a commercial property owner who invests in sustainable building practices or creates welcoming spaces for tenants is demonstrating stewardship on a larger scale. Ownership, in this sense, is not just about control; it's about contribution.

At its heart, ownership in real estate is a balance of rights and responsibilities, entitlement and stewardship. It is both a deeply personal experience and a societal construct, shaped by laws, ethics, and philosophy.

Whether it's a single-family home or a sprawling shopping center, the act of owning property reflects not only the owner's identity but also their values and vision for the world around them.

Conclusion: Entitlement, Stewardship, Legality

This chapter has explored the philosophical and practical dimensions of ownership, revealing how property reflects both rights and responsibilities.

To own something is not just to possess it but to care for it, shape it, and contribute to its broader purpose within a community.

Whether it's a family home that offers shelter and security or a commercial property that fosters growth and opportunity, ownership carries a deeper meaning that extends beyond legal frameworks or financial gains.

As we reflect on what it means to own property, we are naturally drawn to the emotional bonds that ownership creates.

In Chapter 4, we'll delve into these emotional and psychological connections, exploring how feelings like pride, belonging, and nostalgia shape our relationships with the spaces we inhabit.

From the comfort of a cherished home to the ambition tied to a business space, real estate is as much about emotion as it is about structure.

Let's uncover the profound ways in which property resonates with our hearts and minds.

READERS NOTES

CHAPTER 4: Emotional Connection to Real Estate (Entomology)

Exploring the emotional bonds that connect us to the spaces we own and use.

What is Entomology? At its heart, entomology explores the emotional and psychological bonds people form with real estate. It reminds us that property is more than just bricks, mortar, or financial investment, it's deeply personal.

For many, a home isn't merely a shelter; it's a reflection of identity, a source of pride, and a place where memories are created. Similarly, commercial properties often embody the hopes and ambitions of the businesses and individuals they serve.

Emotional connections run deep, shaping decisions that might otherwise appear purely logical.

Imagine a family searching for their first home. While they may focus on practical aspects like the number of bedrooms or proximity to schools, their choice is often guided by something less tangible, a feeling. They might walk into a house and say, "This feels like home." That emotional response often outweighs purely rational considerations, driving them to pursue a property that resonates with their sense of belonging and future aspirations.

In the commercial world, the emotional connection to real estate is no less profound. A small business owner opening their first shop might see the space as more than a location for commerce; it becomes a symbol of their hard work, determination, and ambition. The pride they feel when they unlock the door on opening day is a testament to how deeply personal even commercial spaces can be. A bustling storefront or a thriving office doesn't just represent financial success, it's a place where dreams take shape and grow.

Feelings like nostalgia often play a powerful role in real estate decisions.

A person might hold on to a family home, not because it's the most practical option, but because it's where they grew up, where holidays were celebrated, and where countless memories were created. Letting go of such a property can feel like losing a piece of one's history. Similarly, a commercial building might carry sentimental value for a long-time business owner, representing decades of effort and relationships built within its walls.

Pride is another key emotion tied to real estate.

Owning a home often marks a significant life achievement, providing a sense of accomplishment and stability. For commercial property owners, pride comes from creating spaces that serve a purpose, whether it's a thriving retail hub or a collaborative office environment. These properties aren't just assets; they're legacies that reflect the owner's values and vision.

Belonging is a universal human need, and real estate often provides the foundation for that feeling.

A home offers a personal sanctuary, a place where individuals or families feel safe and rooted. In the commercial realm, spaces like coworking offices or community-centered retail developments foster a sense of connection among users. These spaces become more than locations; they're environments where people come together, share experiences, and build relationships.

Even identity is often tied to real estate.

A home's design, neighborhood, or even its address can reflect how someone sees themselves and how they want to be perceived. In commercial real estate, this can be seen in businesses that choose properties to align with their brand. A sleek, modern office in a bustling city center might signal innovation, while a boutique storefront in a historic district conveys charm and tradition. These choices are rarely just functional, they're expressions of identity.

Emotions and psychology shape every decision, from buying a family home to investing in a commercial property. These connections remind us that real estate is more than a transaction. It's about the spaces where lives unfold, where businesses grow, and where memories are made. By understanding the emotional bonds tied to real estate, we can better appreciate its true value, both as a personal investment and a societal cornerstone.

Conclusion: Pride, Identity, Connection, Memories.

This chapter explored the emotional and psychological connections we form with real estate, revealing how feelings like pride, identity, connection, and memories influence our decisions.

Whether it's the pride of owning a family home, the sense of identity it reflects, the connections it fosters, or the memories it holds, these emotional bonds highlight the deeper meaning behind the properties we own or aspire to own. Similarly, in the commercial real estate world, a thriving retail store or a carefully designed office space can carry profound significance.

These spaces often symbolize the hard work, creativity, and ambition of the people who bring them to life.

They become places where professional identities are forged and connections with employees, customers, and the community are built.

As you reflect on your relationship with real estate, consider how these emotions have shaped your decisions and how they continue to influence the spaces you choose to call yours, whether residential or commercial.

As we've explored the emotional and psychological connections to real estate, it becomes clear that our ties to property are deeply personal and often shaped by intangible forces like pride, identity, and belonging.

Beyond these personal bonds lies a broader framework that governs how spaces are created and managed.

In Chapter 5, we'll turn our focus to the role of politics and governance in shaping the real estate landscape, examining how laws, policies, and philosophical ideals influence the spaces we inhabit.

READERS NOTES

CHAPTER 5: Politics and Governance (Polity)

The philosophical role of governance in shaping real estate landscapes.

What is Polity? At its essence, polity is the framework through which a society organizes itself, governed by laws, policies, and principles that shape how people live and interact. When it comes to real estate, politics and governance form the backbone of how spaces are planned, developed, and maintained.

These frameworks are not just technical or bureaucratic, they are deeply philosophical, rooted in ideas about fairness, justice, and the common good.

In residential real estate, politics and governance are most visible in zoning laws. These regulations determine what can be built and where, shaping neighborhoods and communities in profound ways.

Consider a quiet suburban area designated exclusively for single-family homes.

The zoning reflects a political decision to prioritize privacy, green spaces, and family-oriented living. But what happens when there's pressure to allow higher-density housing to address affordability? The debate over rezoning becomes more than a technical matter, it's a philosophical question about equity, justice, and who gets to belong in a community.

On the commercial side, urban planning illustrates the power of governance to influence real estate. Imagine a city revitalizing its downtown core by incentivizing mixed-use developments, spaces that combine offices, retail, and housing.

Real estate isn't just about economic growth; it's about creating environments that foster connection, accessibility, and innovation.

Yet, these decisions often raise challenging questions. Who benefits from these changes? Do they serve the public good, or do they prioritize the interests of a few?

Governance is tasked with balancing competing needs, and the answers often reveal the underlying philosophy of the policymakers involved.

Taxation is another critical intersection of politics and real estate.

For residential property owners, taxes fund essential services like schools, roads, and public safety, directly impacting their quality of life. But property taxes can also reflect deeper political choices. In some areas, higher taxes on luxury homes aim to promote fairness, redistributing wealth to fund public programs. In commercial real estate, taxation policies can encourage or hinder development.

A tax break for a new business district might spark economic growth, but it also invites questions about fairness.

Should large developers receive incentives while smaller businesses struggle with rising costs? These debates highlight the philosophical tension between fostering growth and ensuring equity.

Governance also plays a crucial role in addressing justice in real estate. Discriminatory practices like redlining, where certain neighborhoods were historically excluded from financial services, show how politics and policies can perpetuate inequality.

Correcting injustices requires political will and a commitment to equity.

For residential real estate, this might mean implementing affordable housing initiatives or fair lending practices. In commercial real estate, it could involve ensuring that underserved areas receive investment, bringing jobs and opportunities to communities long overlooked.

The concept of public spaces reflects the philosophical role of governance in real estate.

Parks, plazas, and community centers are often created through political decisions that prioritize collective well-being over private profit. These spaces foster connection, offering a sense of shared ownership and belonging.

In residential areas, a well-maintained park might become the heart of a neighborhood, while in commercial districts, a pedestrian-friendly plaza could boost foot traffic and local business. Each of these outcomes reflects governance decisions rooted in values like inclusivity and community.

Ultimately, politics and governance are about more than rules, they're about vision.

Every zoning law, tax policy, or urban plan reflects a set of beliefs about what society should look like and how resources should be allocated.

In residential real estate, this might mean ensuring everyone has access to safe, affordable housing. In commercial real estate, it could mean balancing economic development with environmental sustainability.

These decisions are not just practical; they are philosophical, revealing what a society values and aspires to become.

Conclusion: Zoning, Rules, Urban Planning, Taxation

This chapter has explored the philosophical role of governance in shaping real estate, showing how politics and policies influence everything from housing affordability to urban renewal. Whether it's zoning laws that define neighborhoods or tax incentives that drive commercial growth, these decisions reflect deeper ideas about equity, justice, and the common good.

As you reflect on the spaces around you, consider how governance has shaped them, and how it can be used to create more inclusive, equitable, and vibrant communities.

In Chapter 6, we shift our focus to the spatial and relational dynamics of real estate, examining how the design and arrangement of spaces influence human behavior, interactions, and the connections between property and place. Let this perspective expand your understanding of real estate as a system that shapes lives and relationships.

READERS NOTES

CHAPTER 6: Spatial and Relational Dynamics (Typology)

Philosophical insights into the types and relationships of spaces.

What is topology? In essence, topology examines the relationships between spaces and how they interact with one another. In real estate, it's about more than just the physical structures, it's about the connections between these spaces, the dynamics they create, and the roles they play in shaping human behavior and community interactions.

By understanding these spatial and relational dynamics, we can see how real estate reflects and influences the ways we live, work, and connect.

In residential real estate, topology can be observed in how homes are arranged within neighborhoods. Think about a suburban cul-de-sac, where houses face inward, fostering a sense of intimacy and community among neighbors.

Contrast this with an urban apartment building, where dozens of families live side by side but may rarely interact. These different spatial arrangements shape relationships in subtle yet profound ways. One encourages shared experiences and collaboration, while the other prioritizes privacy and independence. Each setup reflects a philosophical decision about how people should relate to the spaces they inhabit and to one another.

Commercial real estate demonstrates topology on a broader scale. Consider a mixed-use development that combines office spaces, retail shops, and residential units in one location. The spatial relationship between these property types creates a dynamic environment where people can live, work, and shop within walking distance.

This type of development prioritizes connectivity and convenience, reflecting a philosophy of integration and efficiency. Yet, it also raises questions:

Does this model strengthen community bonds, or does it prioritize utility over deeper connections? The answer often depends on how the space is designed and used.

Topology also reveals itself in the interplay between property types. A warehouse, for example, may seem purely functional, but its location near major transport routes impacts the surrounding area.

In residential contexts, this could mean noise or increased traffic, challenging the balance between industrial needs and community well-being. In commercial settings, the proximity of such spaces might encourage business growth, providing jobs and economic stability.

These dynamics highlight how the relationships between different types of properties affect both individuals and larger systems.

Philosophically, topology invites us to think about structure and place on a deeper level. A family home isn't just four walls and a roof; it's part of a network of spaces, yards, streets, schools, that create a sense of belonging and security.

Similarly, a commercial building isn't just a place of work; it's a node in a web of economic and social interactions. These spaces don't exist in isolation, they are shaped by their surroundings and, in turn, shape the lives of those who use them.

Understanding these relationships helps us see real estate as a living, interconnected system rather than a collection of isolated properties.

Even the placement of amenities within a community reflects spatial and relational dynamics. A residential neighborhood with parks, schools, and shops nearby fosters a sense of ease and accessibility, enhancing the quality of life for its residents. In commercial districts, the strategic location of coffee shops or restaurants near office buildings can influence how people interact, creating informal spaces for collaboration and networking.

These choices are never random; they are deliberate efforts to balance structure with purpose, reflecting the values of those who design and manage the spaces.

The concept of space also extends beyond the physical. In real estate, relational dynamics often include the intangible connections between people and places. A home might feel welcoming and warm because of its layout and design, but it's also shaped by the relationships within it, family gatherings, quiet evenings, shared meals.

Similarly, a commercial space might thrive not just because of its location but because of the relationships it fosters between clients, employees, and the wider community.

These relational elements are just as important as the physical structures in determining the success and meaning of a space.

Ultimately, topology in real estate is about understanding how spaces and their relationships influence human experiences. Whether it's the design of a family-friendly neighborhood or the layout of a bustling commercial hub, these dynamics shape how we interact with the world around us.

By reflecting on these connections, we can better appreciate the role of real estate in shaping our lives and communities.

Conclusion: Interaction, Connect, Physical, Impact, Dynamics

This chapter has explored the spatial and relational dynamics of real estate, revealing how the design and arrangement of spaces influence human behavior, interactions, and our connections to property.

Whether it's the layout of a neighborhood fostering community bonds or a mixed-use development integrating work and living spaces, these dynamics shape the way we inhabit and experience the world around us.

As we continue this journey, Chapter 7 will guide us into the realm of equality and environmental considerations.

We'll examine how real estate intersects with sustainability and equity, exploring the responsibility we hold to ensure that the spaces we create benefit both people and the planet. Let this next chapter inspire you to think about real estate as part of a larger, more balanced ecosystem.

READERS NOTES

CHAPTER 7: Environmental Considerations (Ecology)

The philosophy of sustainability in real estate.

What is ecology? At its core, ecology is the study of the relationships between living organisms and their environment. When we apply this concept to real estate, it becomes the philosophy of sustainability, an ethical approach to how we design, build, and use spaces while preserving the natural world.

Real estate, whether residential or commercial, doesn't exist in isolation; it is deeply intertwined with the environment, shaping and being shaped by the ecosystems around it.

In residential real estate, sustainability often starts with green building practices.

Consider a family constructing a home with solar panels, energy-efficient insulation, and rainwater harvesting systems. These decisions reflect more than just cost-saving measures, they are a statement of responsibility toward the planet.

The family isn't just creating a home for themselves; they're contributing to a broader effort to reduce carbon footprints and live in harmony with nature. It's a reflection of how individual choices in real estate can align with larger ecological values.

In commercial real estate, sustainability often takes on a larger scale. Picture a modern office building with a LEED certification, designed to maximize natural light, minimize energy consumption, and incorporate green roofs that reduce urban heat.

This kind of development goes beyond meeting market demands; it demonstrates a commitment to environmental stewardship.

Developers and property owners in this sphere aren't just building structures, they're setting examples of how commercial spaces can adapt to ecological needs without compromising functionality or appeal.

Environmental considerations also raise questions of equity, which tie back to earlier chapters like Value and Worth and Politics and Governance.

Who benefits from green spaces, and how are these benefits distributed? In residential real estate, neighborhoods with parks, tree-lined streets, and clean air often come at a premium, pricing out many families who would equally benefit from these ecological advantages.

Similarly, in commercial real estate, sustainable developments may attract higher rents, making them inaccessible to smaller businesses. These scenarios highlight the importance of ensuring that sustainability isn't just a luxury but a standard accessible to all.

Urban planning plays a critical role in bridging ecology and real estate, blending the philosophical with the practical. In residential contexts, this might involve designing walkable neighborhoods that reduce dependence on cars, fostering healthier lifestyles while lowering emissions.

In commercial spaces, it could mean creating business districts with robust public transit options, connecting workers to their jobs efficiently while minimizing environmental impact. These choices reflect a balance of responsibility, to both the planet and the people who inhabit these spaces.

Reflecting on earlier chapters, we see how environmental considerations overlap with ideas explored in Ownership and Rights.

Stewardship is as much about caring for the environment as it is about maintaining the property itself.

A family maintaining a home garden or a commercial developer preserving wetlands near a construction site embodies the idea that real estate owners are caretakers, not just for their land but for the ecosystems their land is part of.

Even the emotional connections discussed in *Emotional Connection to Real Estate* play a role here. People often form bonds with natural spaces, a tree in the backyard, a view of the mountains, or a community park.

These connections aren't just sentimental; they're a reminder of our deep reliance on and responsibility toward the natural world.

Real estate, whether residential or commercial, becomes a bridge between humanity and the environment, blending structure with the beauty and necessity of nature.

The responsibility of integrating sustainability into real estate lies with everyone, developers, owners, planners, and even tenants.

A home equipped with green technology or a commercial property designed for environmental efficiency isn't just a space to occupy; it's a statement about the kind of future we want to build. Real estate is not just an industry; it's a participant in the global effort to preserve and respect the environment while meeting the needs of those who inhabit it.

Conclusion: Environment, Ethics, Responsibility, Conservation.

This chapter has explored the ecological philosophy of real estate, blending ethical responsibility with practical applications like green building and urban planning. From the sustainable design of a family home to a commercial building that reduces its carbon footprint, we see how real estate can embrace the principles of ecology.

These considerations also echo earlier chapters, tying together ideas of worth, ownership, and connection in a way that emphasizes our shared responsibility toward the planet.

In the next chapter, we'll explore the cultural and social constructs that shape real estate, diving into how societal norms and values influence property trends and community development.

Let this reflection on sustainability and equity inspire you to see real estate as part of a larger ecosystem, one where the balance between human need and environmental care defines the spaces we create.

READERS NOTES

CHAPTER 8: Cultural and Social Constructs (Sociology)

The cultural philosophy behind real estate trends and societal norms.

What is sociology? At its core, sociology is the study of human behavior within groups and societies, exploring the norms, values, and structures that shape how people interact. When applied to real estate, sociology reveals how cultural philosophies and social constructs influence the spaces we create, inhabit, and transform.

Real estate, whether residential or commercial, doesn't exist in isolation, it is a reflection of societal trends, values, and aspirations, constantly evolving with the communities it serves.

In residential real estate, sociology is evident in how neighborhoods are formed and shaped by cultural preferences.

Think about the evolution of suburban communities, where single-family homes with spacious yards reflect a cultural ideal of privacy and family life. These areas were often built on the belief that such environments foster stability and prosperity.

However, as societal norms shift toward prioritizing sustainability and accessibility, urban living has become more appealing, reflecting a new cultural trend that values walkability, shared spaces, and reduced environmental impact. These shifting preferences highlight how social constructs continuously redefine what we consider desirable in a home.

In commercial real estate, sociology plays an equally critical role. Consider how the design of shopping centers, office spaces, or coworking hubs reflects societal trends. For decades, sprawling malls dominated retail culture, symbolizing convenience and consumerism.

Today, as online shopping grows, retail spaces are adapting to meet the demand for experiences rather than just transactions. Similarly, coworking spaces have emerged as a response to changing work norms, emphasizing flexibility, collaboration, and community over traditional corporate environments.

These shifts illustrate how commercial spaces adapt to evolving cultural and social expectations.

The concept of community cohesion is central to both residential and commercial spaces. In residential neighborhoods, strong community ties are often fostered by shared spaces such as parks, schools, and community centers. These spaces are designed not just to serve practical needs but to encourage interaction and a sense of belonging. For example, a neighborhood park might bring together families, joggers, and dog walkers, creating a microcosm of social connections.

In commercial settings, spaces like open-air markets or pedestrian-friendly plazas similarly encourage interaction, fostering connections between businesses and their customers while reinforcing the sense of a vibrant, interconnected community.

Gentrification is another powerful example of sociology's impact on real estate.

In residential areas, the redevelopment of urban neighborhoods often brings new investment, improved infrastructure, and rising property values. However, it also raises complex social questions about displacement, inequality, and cultural preservation.

For some, gentrification represents progress, while for others, it signals a loss of identity and community.

In commercial real estate, similar tensions arise when new developments replace older, culturally significant spaces. The challenge lies in balancing growth with the preservation of community character and ensuring that progress doesn't come at the cost of social cohesion.

Social constructs also influence housing markets in subtle but profound ways.

Cultural ideals about success and status often shape demand for certain property types. A large home in an exclusive neighborhood might symbolize achievement, while a modern apartment in a trendy urban area could reflect a lifestyle centered on convenience and connection.

In commercial spaces, businesses often choose locations that align with their brand image, seeking areas that resonate with their target audience. These decisions, guided by societal values, show how deeply real estate is intertwined with cultural and social identity.

Philosophy underpins all these interactions, encouraging us to question not just what we build but why we build it. Residential developments that prioritize affordability over exclusivity or commercial spaces designed for inclusivity rather than elitism reflect philosophical choices about the kind of society we want to create.

Real estate is more than a response to societal trends, it actively shapes them, influencing how communities grow and evolve over time.

As we reflect on these ideas, it becomes clear that real estate is not just about physical spaces but about the people who inhabit and interact with them. The sociology of real estate reminds us that every home, office, or store is part of a larger social fabric, shaped by the values, norms, and aspirations of its time.

Understanding these dynamics allows us to approach real estate with greater awareness of its role in building and sustaining communities.

Conclusion: Trends, Community, Cohesion, Gentrification.

This chapter has examined the cultural and social constructs that shape real estate, from the evolving preferences of residential neighborhoods to the adaptive designs of commercial spaces. It has shown how societal norms and values influence housing markets, urban development, and community cohesion.

As you reflect on the spaces you encounter daily, consider how they embody the cultural trends and social philosophies of their time.

In the next chapter, we will explore the human relationship with habitation and space, delving into the anthropology of real estate. Together, we'll uncover how the spaces we occupy reflect our deepest needs for identity, belonging, and evolution.

Let this journey deepen your understanding of real estate as more than property, it is a living, breathing expression of human culture and connection.

READERS NOTES

CHAPTER 9: Habitation and Space (Anthropology)

Philosophical reflections on human habitation and the need for shelter.

What is anthropology? At its essence, anthropology is the study of humans, their cultures, behaviors, and the ways they interact with their environments. When applied to real estate, it becomes a lens through which we explore the profound relationship between people and the spaces they inhabit.

Real estate, whether residential or commercial, is not merely a collection of properties; it is a reflection of humanity's need for shelter, identity, and connection. It tells the story of who we are and how we evolve within the spaces we call our own.

In residential real estate, habitation begins with the simplest of needs, shelter.

A house is not just a structure but a sanctuary, a place where people seek safety and comfort. It becomes a home when it reflects the identity of those who live within it.

Think of a young family moving into their first home. The bare walls soon carry pictures of milestones, the garden echoes with laughter, and the space transforms into an extension of their lives. This is habitation in its truest form, a blend of physical space and emotional connection.

Commercial real estate also mirrors human habitation, albeit on a broader scale. A well-designed office building doesn't just provide desks and chairs; it creates an environment where people come together to collaborate and innovate. Consider a bustling coworking space.

It is more than a workplace; it is a hub of energy, fostering a sense of belonging among individuals from different industries. This idea of commercial habitation reflects humanity's inherent need to connect, adapt, and thrive within shared spaces.

As we trace the evolution of human habitation, we see how it reflects philosophical ideals of identity and belonging.

Early communities were built around shared resources, with homes clustered together for mutual support and safety. Modern residential neighborhoods, though often more fragmented, still carry echoes of this communal spirit in shared spaces like parks and schools.

Commercial developments, too, are shaped by these ideals. Shopping centers, for instance, are not merely transactional hubs but places where communities gather, interact, and form connections.

The relationship between space and identity ties back to concepts explored in earlier chapters, like *Spatial and Relational Dynamics* and *Emotional Connection to Real Estate.*

A home's design can reflect the personality of its owner, just as the layout of a commercial building can convey the values of the businesses it houses.

These spaces do not exist in isolation, they are shaped by the people who inhabit them, and in turn, they shape the experiences and aspirations of those who use them.

Shelter, at its core, is one of humanity's most fundamental needs.

Yet, it is also deeply philosophical. Residential spaces must balance practicality with emotional resonance, offering not just a roof but a sense of belonging. Commercial spaces, on the other hand, must meet the needs of their users while contributing to the broader community.

A restaurant in a busy urban district may serve food, but it also becomes a gathering place where stories are shared and connections are forged. Similarly, a residential development with thoughtfully designed communal areas fosters relationships among neighbors, enhancing the sense of community.

Habitation also reflects the evolution of communities.

In residential real estate, this evolution is visible in the shift from rural villages to sprawling suburbs and, more recently, to compact urban developments.

Each stage tells a story of changing human priorities, from the need for space to the desire for proximity and convenience. Commercial spaces mirror this progression, evolving from standalone stores to integrated mixed-use developments that blend work, leisure, and living spaces. These shifts reflect how habitation adapts to the changing needs of individuals and societies.

Real estate is, in many ways, an ongoing dialogue between people and the spaces they inhabit.

Residential properties tell the stories of individuals and families, while commercial properties speak to the collective ambitions of businesses and communities.

By understanding the philosophical underpinnings of habitation and space, we gain a deeper appreciation of how real estate shapes and is shaped by the human experience.

Conclusion: Shelter, Design, Identity, Evolution, Belonging.

This chapter has traced the profound relationship between habitation and space, revealing how the places we occupy reflect our identity, belonging, and community evolution. Whether it's the personal sanctuary of a home or the shared energy of a commercial space, real estate is a canvas for human life.

These connections echo themes from earlier chapters, like the emotional bonds of ownership and the interplay of space and relationships, tying them together with the universal need for shelter.

In the next chapter, we will explore the transformative impacts of technology on real estate, examining how innovation reshapes the spaces we inhabit and the way we interact with them. Let this reflection on habitation inspire you to consider how the spaces around you contribute to your sense of self and community.

READERS NOTES

CHAPTER 10: Transformative Impacts and Trends (Technology)

The philosophy of innovation in reshaping real estate.

What is technology? For most of us it is the devices we use, the systems we rely on, and the tools that shape our daily lives. But in the context of philosophy, technology is more than just functionality; it is a force of innovation that challenges the way we think, live, and interact.

When applied to real estate, technology becomes a transformative power, reshaping how we conceive of and engage with the spaces around us. It forces us to reflect on progress and adaptation, not just in terms of what we build, but how and why we build it.

In residential real estate, technology has redefined the meaning of "home."

Smart homes, for instance, are no longer futuristic concepts, they are here, integrating devices and systems that respond to our needs in real time. Imagine a family that can control their lighting, security, and climate systems from their phones, creating an environment tailored to their comfort and convenience.

This is not just about efficiency; it's a reflection of how we've come to expect spaces to adapt to us. Philosophically, it raises questions about autonomy, dependence, and how far technology should influence the most personal aspects of our lives.

In the commercial realm, the transformative impact of technology is equally profound. Consider coworking spaces that rely on apps to manage bookings, offer virtual access, and connect users within a global network. These spaces are more than offices; they are hubs of innovation, enabling businesses to operate with unprecedented flexibility.

Blockchain technology, too, has entered the commercial real estate landscape, streamlining transactions and providing transparency in ways that were unimaginable just a decade ago. Yet, with this progress comes the question: does technology enhance human connections in these spaces, or does it risk replacing them with automation and data?

The balance between progress and preservation is a recurring theme in real estate, as seen in earlier chapters like Ownership and Rights and Environmental Considerations.

Just as ownership carries responsibilities and sustainability demands balance, technology's role in real estate must also be carefully managed. In residential spaces, for example, the convenience of smart home technology often comes with privacy concerns. Who controls the data collected by these systems, and how might that affect our sense of security? Similarly, in commercial real estate, the efficiency brought by automation could risk sidelining the human elements that make these spaces vibrant and meaningful.

Philosophy encourages us to view technology not as a standalone phenomenon but as a tool that interacts with broader societal trends.

This ties back to *Social Constructs,* where we discussed how cultural values shape real estate. Technology, influenced by these values, often mirrors societal priorities. For example, sustainable technologies like solar panels or energy-efficient systems reflect a growing cultural emphasis on environmental stewardship.

By embedding these advancements into residential and commercial spaces, we see a convergence of technology and philosophy, each shaping the other.

Looking forward, technology in real estate prompts us to imagine the spaces of the future.

Smart cities, for instance, are no longer distant dreams, they are actively being built, integrating technology to manage everything from traffic to energy consumption. These advancements extend beyond individual homes or offices, creating interconnected systems that redefine what it means to live and work in harmony with our surroundings.

Yet, as with all progress, there are trade-offs. How do we ensure that these spaces remain inclusive, accessible, and meaningful for everyone? This question bridges the philosophical and the practical, reminding us that technology, like real estate, is ultimately about people.

The transformative power of technology is not just about what is possible, it's about what is desirable.

For a homeowner, the decision to integrate smart technology might reflect a desire for convenience or sustainability. For a commercial developer, adopting blockchain systems could signal a commitment to transparency and efficiency.

Both choices are philosophical as much as they are practical, reflecting values that extend beyond the immediate benefits of innovation. These decisions show how technology doesn't just change real estate; it redefines the way we relate to it.

As we consider the spaces we inhabit, whether residential or commercial, it's essential to view technology not as an external force but as an integrated part of the human experience.

It shapes how we interact with our surroundings and how we envision the future.

Just as previous chapters have highlighted themes of connection, ownership, and responsibility, technology weaves these ideas together, offering new opportunities while challenging us to consider their implications.

Conclusion: Progress, Adaptation, Transformation, Connection.

This chapter has explored the transformative impacts of technology on real estate, from smart homes that adapt to our needs to commercial systems that streamline global operations. These innovations, though powerful, invite us to reflect on the philosophical questions of progress, adaptation, and human connection.

As we look to the future of real estate, technology will continue to shape the spaces we inhabit, offering both possibilities and challenges.

In the next chapter, we'll examine the economic forces that drive real estate, exploring how market dynamics intersect with philosophical ideas of scarcity, opportunity, and value. Let this reflection on technology inspire you to think not just about what we build but how we adapt, innovate, and progress within the spaces we call our own.

READERS NOTES

CHAPTER 11: Market Forces (Economy)

Philosophical underpinnings of market forces in real estate.

What are market forces in the economy? At its core, an economy is a system that governs how resources are produced, distributed, and consumed, with market forces driving the dynamics of supply, demand, and value within this framework.

But when we consider it through a philosophical lens, the economy becomes a reflection of human behavior, choices, and values.

In real estate, the economy isn't just a backdrop, it's a dynamic force that drives the market, shaping everything from where people live to how businesses thrive. It's about the constant interplay of supply, demand, scarcity, and opportunity, creating a rhythm that dictates how spaces are created, exchanged, and valued.

In residential real estate, the forces of supply and demand are often deeply personal. Picture a growing city where families are searching for homes close to schools and work. When the supply of homes cannot keep pace with demand, prices rise, creating competition that can feel both exciting and daunting. These market forces are not just numbers, they represent human aspirations and the pursuit of belonging. Philosophically, this scarcity challenges us to think about fairness, access, and the balance between individual desires and collective needs.

In commercial real estate, the stakes are just as high, though the dynamics can differ. Consider a bustling retail district where businesses compete for prime locations. The limited availability of high-traffic properties creates opportunities for some while presenting barriers for others.

These forces reflect not only economic principles but also philosophical ideas about opportunity and merit. Who gets access to the best spaces, and what does that say about the values of the market?

Questions like this connect to earlier chapters, such as Politics and Governance, which examined how policies influence access, equity, and the broader dynamics of real estate.

Scarcity, a central theme in economic philosophy, plays a profound role in real estate. In residential markets, limited land availability often pushes developers to build vertically, creating high-rise apartments in urban areas. This scarcity influences not only the price of property but also the way people experience their homes. For some, it's an opportunity to live in vibrant city centers; for others, it raises questions about space, privacy, and quality of life.

Commercial markets face similar challenges, where the scarcity of land in central business districts forces businesses to innovate, such as creating shared workspaces or investing in suburban hubs.

Opportunity, the flip side of scarcity, reveals how markets can drive innovation and progress. Residential neighborhoods that were once overlooked can become highly sought after as trends shift, offering opportunities for growth and investment.

Similarly, in commercial real estate, emerging technologies like blockchain have created new avenues for transparency and efficiency, as discussed in *Transformative Impacts*.

These innovations don't just solve problems; they reflect the philosophical idea that challenges can be catalysts for growth, shaping the future of real estate.

The relationship between economy and real estate also ties back to earlier chapters, like *Value and Worth,* where we explored the intrinsic and extrinsic aspects of property. Economic forces often emphasize the extrinsic, focusing on market value, investment potential, and financial returns. However, the intrinsic value of real estate, its ability to provide shelter, foster community, and enhance quality of life, remains equally vital.

This balance between financial considerations and human needs creates a dynamic tension that defines the real estate market.

As we move forward, the economy's influence on real estate will only grow more complex. The integration of sustainability, as discussed in *Environmental Considerations,* adds another layer to market dynamics. For example, residential properties with eco-friendly features often command higher prices, reflecting a shift in societal values toward conservation.

In commercial markets, companies that prioritize green building standards may gain a competitive edge, appealing to environmentally conscious clients and consumers.

These trends highlight how the economy is not just reactive, it's a reflection of evolving cultural and philosophical priorities.

Real estate markets are, at their core, a mirror of human behavior.

They reveal what we value, what we aspire to, and how we adapt to challenges. Residential and commercial properties are not just commodities, they are integral to the economy's story, representing both scarcity and opportunity.

By understanding the philosophical underpinnings of market forces, we can navigate these dynamics with greater awareness, appreciating not just the numbers but the human stories behind them.

Conclusion: Scarcity, Opportunity, Supply, Demand, Fairness, Trends.

This chapter has explored the economic principles that drive real estate, from the scarcity of land to the opportunities created by shifting markets.

Residential and commercial spaces alike are shaped by the interplay of supply, demand, and human values.

These forces connect deeply with earlier themes, such as worth, governance, and transformation, tying them into a broader understanding of the market as a living, evolving system.

In the next chapter, we will delve into the concept of spatial identity, exploring how the places we inhabit shape who we are and how we connect with the world.

Let this reflection on the economy inspire you to see real estate not just as a market but as a dynamic force that bridges human needs and aspirations.

READERS NOTES

CHAPTER 12: Spatial Identity, Place, and Self (Topology)

The philosophy of place and its impact on identity.

What is topology? In its simplest form, topology is the study of relationships between spaces, exploring how the physical and the abstract intersect to create meaning. In real estate, topology takes on a philosophical dimension as it examines how places shape identity and how individuals and communities, in turn, define the spaces they inhabit.

From the way a home reflects personal values to the design of a commercial hub that fosters connection, real estate becomes a stage for the interplay between self and place.

In residential real estate, the relationship between space and identity often begins with the home.

A family house, for example, is more than just a structure; it becomes a reflection of the people who live there. Its design, decor, and location all contribute to a sense of belonging and personal expression. Whether it's a small apartment in a vibrant city or a quiet house in the suburbs, the space embodies the aspirations and lifestyle of its inhabitants, grounding them in a physical sense of self.

Commercial real estate plays a similar role but on a broader scale. A well-designed office building or retail space is often crafted with the identity of its users in mind. Consider a sleek corporate headquarters in a bustling urban district. Its towering glass facade doesn't just house employees; it signals innovation and ambition.

Conversely, a boutique store nestled in a historic neighborhood reflects charm and tradition, creating an emotional connection with customers and the community.

These spaces don't just meet functional needs, they tell stories about the people and values they represent.

The philosophy of place becomes even more profound when considering community connections. In residential neighborhoods, shared spaces like parks, schools, and libraries create a sense of unity, allowing individuals to feel part of something larger than themselves. These communal areas reinforce the idea that space is not just personal but collective, weaving individual lives into a shared identity.

Similarly, commercial developments like shopping centers or coworking spaces provide opportunities for collaboration and interaction, building networks that extend beyond the walls of any one property.

This concept ties back to earlier discussions, such as *Emotional Connection to Real Estate,* where we explored how feelings like belonging and pride are deeply connected to the spaces we inhabit. Topology takes this further by focusing on how geography and spatial relationships shape those emotions, turning individual attachments into broader communal bonds.

Whether it's a family planting roots in a neighborhood or a business integrating into a local economy, the dynamic between place and identity remains central to the real estate experience.

In many ways, the geography of a space plays as much a role in shaping identity as the structure itself.

A home overlooking a serene lake may foster feelings of tranquility and reflection, while a commercial property in a busy city square exudes energy and purpose. These environments influence how people perceive themselves and interact with their surroundings, blending the physical and the philosophical into a unified sense of place.

Even as technology reshapes how we engage with real estate, the importance of spatial identity endures. Smart homes and virtual workplaces may introduce convenience and adaptability, but they also challenge us to redefine what it means to be rooted in a place.

These innovations, as discussed in *Transformative Impacts,* offer opportunities to expand our relationships with space while reminding us of the enduring need for meaningful connections to our environments.

Ultimately, real estate is about more than buildings and markets, it's about the relationship between people and the places they inhabit. Residential and commercial spaces alike act as canvases for self-expression and community building, reflecting the identities of those who shape and are shaped by them.

By understanding the philosophical ties between self and place, we gain deeper insight into how real estate influences the human experience by shaping our sense of identity, belonging, and purpose. These connections are not merely functional or aesthetic; they are deeply rooted in our emotions and values.

A home becomes a sanctuary that reflects who we are, while a workplace or commercial space aligns with how we contribute to society and interact with others.

Real estate, in this way, serves as a bridge between our internal world and the external environment, fostering connections that influence how we see ourselves and our role within a community. It allows us to explore how physical spaces impact our personal growth, relationships, and sense of belonging, making the spaces we inhabit integral to our understanding of life itself.

Conclusion: Geography, Community, Self, Personal, Communal, Feelings, Design, Structure.

This chapter has explored the profound connection between spatial identity and real estate, showing how places shape our sense of self and our ties to the community.

Whether through the comfort of a family home or the energy of a bustling commercial hub, these spaces reflect the intricate relationship between geography, identity, and belonging.

As we move forward, the next chapter will delve into the interconnectedness of real estate on a global scale, examining how local and international markets influence one another.

Let this reflection on the personal and communal aspects of space inspire you to consider the broader connections that real estate creates across the world.

READERS NOTES

CHAPTER 13: Market Interconnectivity and Systems (Globality)

The philosophical implications of global real estate connections.

What is Globality? At its core, Globality represents the seamless interconnection of global markets, a concept that mirrors the flow of capital, ideas, and resources across borders. In the realm of real estate, it's a philosophical exploration of how local and global systems intertwine, shaping properties and investments in ways that transcend geography.

As globalization connects markets more tightly than ever, real estate becomes a reflection of shared values, aspirations, and trends on a global stage.

In residential real estate, Globality can be seen in the rise of international property investments. Think of families purchasing vacation homes in foreign countries or expatriates seeking homes abroad.

These transactions go far beyond personal preferences and they do reflect a larger growing interconnectedness, where markets influence each other across continents.

A booming housing market in one region might draw investors from another, demonstrating how global trends ripple through local markets.

Philosophically, this raises questions about belonging, ownership, and the cultural exchange embedded in property transactions.

Commercial real estate exemplifies this interconnectedness even more starkly. Consider global corporations establishing regional headquarters in key cities worldwide. A technology company in Silicon Valley might set up an office in Singapore to tap into Asia's growing market, bringing with it not just jobs but a cultural and economic footprint.

These decisions are influenced by global market trends, trade policies, and economic forecasts, highlighting the systems and values that drive real estate decisions on a macro scale. Yet, they also invite philosophical reflection:

How do these global movements shape local economies, communities, and identities?

As we near the end of this book, it's important to reflect on how the themes of earlier chapters, such as *Market Forces* and *Spatial Identity, Place, and Self*, interact with Globality. Markets are no longer confined to specific regions; they are part of a larger, fluid network where supply, demand, and opportunity are shaped by global factors.

Similarly, our sense of place and identity is influenced by this global connectivity. A home or office space today might be designed with influences from multiple cultures, blending styles and functions to reflect the diverse needs of its occupants.

If you're intrigued by the economic foundations of this global interconnectedness, I invite you to explore my book, *Capital Markets and Real Estate: Bridging Markets for a Global Future.*

There, you'll find a deeper dive into the economic principles and financial systems that drive these trends, offering a comprehensive look at how markets function on a global scale. While this chapter focuses on the philosophical and practical implications for real estate, the *Capital Markets* book expands the conversation to include the intricate mechanics of international finance and investment.

Globality also reminds us that real estate is a shared system.

Residential and commercial properties alike exist within networks of trade, technology, and cultural exchange. A luxury apartment in London might be influenced by design trends from Dubai, while a retail space in New York City could serve as a hub for products sourced from across the globe.

These connections are not just economic, they represent a shared understanding of value, quality, and purpose that transcends borders.

As globalization continues to shape the world, it challenges us to think about the ethical and practical implications of interconnected markets. Who benefits from these global flows, and who is left behind?

In residential real estate, for example, foreign investment can drive up housing prices, making homes less accessible to local residents. In commercial real estate, the influx of international businesses can revitalize a city's economy but also disrupt local industries. These complexities highlight the importance of balancing global ambition with local responsibility.

Ultimately, Globality in real estate reflects the broader human experience of connection and exchange.

Just as people move across borders, bringing their values, skills, and ideas, so too does real estate evolve in response to these flows.

By understanding the philosophical ties between global systems and local spaces, we can better appreciate the role of real estate in bridging cultures, economies, and communities.

Conclusion and Call to Action

As we near the conclusion of this book, this chapter has explored how globalization shapes real estate through interconnected systems and shared values. From the cross-border purchase of homes to the establishment of global business hubs, Globality demonstrates how real estate reflects and contributes to a world that is increasingly interconnected. The global economy can be seen almost like a suburb growing into a city, then expanding into a state, a country, multiple countries, continents, and ultimately encompassing the entire Earth.

These themes tie into earlier discussions of market forces and identity, highlighting the complex web of influences that shape the spaces we inhabit.

In the next chapter, we'll step back to reflect on housing philosophy and societal reflections, exploring how real estate embodies deeper ideals of equality and dignity. Let this reflection on global connectivity inspire you to think of real estate not just as property but as part of a global story that connects us all.

READERS NOTES

CHAPTER 14: Housing Philosophy Societal Reflections

Philosophical reflections on housing as a societal cornerstone.

What is housing philosophy? As it relates to real estate, housing philosophy is the study of housing as a fundamental societal cornerstone. It considers housing as more than a physical structure, it's a fundamental human need that reflects broader ideals of equality, dignity, and community.

From the smallest home to the largest commercial development, the spaces we create and inhabit reveal the values and priorities of our societies.

Housing shapes how we live, interact, and connect, making it an integral part of the human experience.

In residential real estate, housing fulfills one of humanity's most basic needs: shelter. But it doesn't stop there. A home becomes a symbol of stability and belonging, a place where families create memories and individuals find respite from the world.

Imagine a modest house in a growing community, its walls may be simple, but they hold the dreams of those who live there. It's a space where dignity is preserved, and equality can begin to take shape, providing a foundation for a better future.

This philosophical reflection reminds us that housing is more than property; it's a representation of societal values.

Commercial real estate, though often perceived as driven by profit, also carries a societal role. Consider a mixed-use development in an urban area. It might house businesses, provide jobs, and offer spaces for social gathering, such as cafes or public plazas.

These developments embody a philosophy of inclusivity, creating environments where people from diverse backgrounds can coexist and thrive.

The design and function of such spaces reflect not only economic opportunity but also the ideals of dignity and equality within a community. They are a testament to how commercial spaces can contribute to the social fabric of a city.

Housing, whether residential or commercial, has always been a reflection of society's evolution.

In earlier chapters, we explored how concepts like *Ownership and Rights* and *Spatial Identity* influence our relationship with property. Housing philosophy ties these themes together by focusing on the shared human need for shelter and the societal implications of meeting that need.

A family's struggle to afford a home in a competitive market mirrors a small business's challenge to secure a retail space in a thriving district. Both situations highlight the tension between equality and opportunity, underscoring the philosophical importance of accessible housing for all.

The dignity tied to housing becomes even more profound when we consider marginalized communities.

Residential developments that prioritize affordable housing signal a commitment to equity, ensuring that homes are not just for the privileged but for everyone. In the commercial sector, community-focused projects, such as local marketplaces or coworking spaces for small businesses, can empower those who might otherwise be excluded.

These examples show how real estate can foster inclusion and uphold societal values of fairness and respect.

At its heart, housing philosophy prompts us to ask what kind of society we want to create through the spaces we build.

A home is not just a roof over one's head; it's a cornerstone of security and identity.

Similarly, a commercial property is not just a venue for transactions, it's a place where people come together, exchange ideas, and grow collectively. Spaces are reflections of our shared commitment to ensuring that everyone has a chance to live with dignity and purpose.

Looking ahead, housing philosophy challenges us to think about the future of housing in both residential and commercial contexts. As technology and globalization continue to shape real estate, the question remains: how can we balance progress with the principles of equality and community?

This reflection ties back to themes of *Environmental Considerations* and *Globality,* reminding us that the spaces we create must serve not just the present but also future generations.

The philosophy of housing is, in many ways, the philosophy of humanity itself, a reminder that the spaces we inhabit are a testament to our collective values.

Conclusion: Dignity, Equality, Exclusion, Inclusion, Progress

This chapter has explored housing as a societal cornerstone, highlighting how spaces reflect our deepest commitments to equality, dignity, and community. From the personal sanctuary of a home to the shared energy of commercial spaces, real estate embodies the ideals of society, shaping how we live and connect. These reflections echo earlier themes, such as identity and global connectivity, while pointing us toward the future.

In the final chapter, we'll bring all these ideas together, reflecting on the journey of real estate through a philosophical lens and considering its evolution in the years to come. Let this chapter inspire you to view housing not just as a necessity but as a vital part of the human story, one that connects us all.

READERS NOTES

CHAPTER 15: Summation - Real Estate, Philosophy, and the Path Ahead

Reflecting on the philosophical journey of real estate.

As we reach the end of this journey, it's time to reflect on the philosophical exploration of real estate that began at the very first chapter. This book has delved into concepts that extend far beyond bricks and mortar, revealing the intricate relationship between property and human values, aspirations, and connections.

Together, we've uncovered the ways in which residential and commercial real estate embody deeper principles of identity, community, and progress, shaping not only the spaces we inhabit but also the lives we lead.

At its heart, real estate is a reflection of human philosophy.

In *Introduction to Philosophy and Real Estate,* we began by grounding our understanding in the fundamental interplay between abstract ideas and tangible spaces.

From there, *Value and Worth* examined how intrinsic and extrinsic values influence decisions about property, while *Ownership and Rights* highlighted the responsibilities and privileges tied to ownership.

These themes are more than theoretical, they inform everyday decisions about where and how we live and work.

As we moved through chapters like *Spatial Identity, Place, and Self* and *Emotional Connection to Real Estate,* we explored how spaces shape us and how we, in turn, define those spaces.

Residential properties become more than homes, they evolve into sanctuaries of belonging and pride. Similarly, commercial spaces transcend transactions, fostering collaboration and innovation. These ideas are central to understanding the essence of real estate as both a personal and societal construct.

The interconnectedness of global markets, explored in *Globality,* and the pressing need for sustainable practices in *Environmental Considerations,* have shown how real estate reflects broader global trends.

Whether it's a green-certified building attracting tenants with a shared commitment to the environment or a commercial hub influenced by international investment, these examples illustrate how the principles of philosophy and practicality intertwine in real estate decisions.

The philosophy of housing as a societal cornerstone, brought to light the enduring importance of shelter in fostering dignity, equality, and inclusion. This chapter tied together the human and societal elements of real estate, bridging the gap between the personal spaces we cherish and the shared environments that build community. Whether it's an affordable housing initiative in a residential area or a coworking space designed to empower small businesses, real estate has the power to uplift individuals and transform societies.

Throughout this book, we've returned time and again to the importance of balance, between progress and tradition, individuality and community, the local and the global.

Real estate exists at the intersection of these forces, constantly adapting to meet the needs of a changing world. Technology, discussed in *Transformative Impacts,* plays a key role in this evolution, reshaping both residential and commercial spaces in ways that challenge and inspire.

As you reflect on this journey, consider how the themes of this book apply to your own experiences with real estate.

Whether you're a homeowner, an investor, or a professional in the industry, the philosophical insights explored here offer a lens through which to view the spaces around you. Real estate is more than a market, it's a living philosophy, a testament to humanity's ability to create, connect, and adapt.

Looking to the future, the evolution of real estate will continue to reflect the values and priorities of society.

The challenges of affordability, sustainability, and global interconnectedness require thoughtful solutions, rooted in the principles we've explored.

At the same time, opportunities abound for innovation and growth, offering new ways to bridge the tangible and the philosophical in real estate.

Conclusion: Property, People, Ideas, Spaces

This chapter has brought together the themes of this book, reflecting on the philosophical journey of real estate and envisioning the path ahead.

From the foundational concepts of value and ownership to the transformative impacts of technology and globalization, we've explored how real estate shapes and is shaped by the human experience.

As you close this book, let it serve as a reminder that real estate is not just about property, it's about people, ideas, and the spaces that connect us.

Let these insights inspire you to think critically and creatively about the role of real estate in your own life and in the broader world.

The journey doesn't end here; it's a foundation for your next steps, filled with understanding, confidence, and purpose.

I want to take this moment to wish you all the best as you move forward, equipped with the knowledge and insights gained from this journey. Thank you for taking the time to read and reflect on the philosophy of real estate, on the people, the spaces, and the values that shape this ever-evolving market.

May this book inspire you to see real estate not just as a collection of properties, but as a living, breathing reflection of humanity and its aspirations. May your journey be one of purpose, property and people.

Willem Tait

READERS NOTES

Glossary

This glossary brings together the core ideas that link philosophy and real estate. Concepts of value, ownership, space, ethics, and human behavior.

My hope is that you'll carry some of these ideas into your daily thinking and allow them to shape your real estate strategy and perspective.

Axiology (Value and Worth): The philosophical study of value. In real estate, it explores why people assign worth to property, balancing emotional, ethical, and market-based measures.

Anthropology (Habitation and Belonging): The study of human life and culture. In property, it explains how our need for shelter, identity, and continuity shapes the spaces we build and inhabit.

Ecology (Sustainability and Responsibility): The relationship between people, property, and environment. It reminds us that development carries a duty to conserve resources and design for long-term balance.

Economy (Market Forces and Fairness): The system of exchange that determines property value. Philosophically, it asks how markets can serve both opportunity and justice.

Entomology (Emotional Connection): The study of our emotional bonds with places. It shows how pride, memory, and identity influence the value we place on homes and buildings.

Ethics (Integrity and Stewardship): The moral foundation of real estate. It calls for fairness, transparency, and responsibility in ownership, development, and investment.

Globality (Interconnected Markets): The interdependence of local and global real estate systems. Philosophically, it represents how shared values, cultures, and economies link our spaces and societies.

Governance (Polity and Regulation): The framework of laws, zoning, and policy that shape property rights and community growth. Philosophically, it reflects how order, justice, and authority guide our built environment.

Habitation (Living and Meaning): The act of dwelling within space. It joins the physical reality of shelter with the emotional and existential need to belong.

Ontology (Ownership and Being): The philosophy of existence and possession. In real estate, it asks what it means to *own* something and how ownership defines identity and responsibility.

Perception (Value and Experience): The lens through which people interpret property and place. Market value often begins in perception, influenced by trust, emotion, and presentation.

Philosophy (Meaning and Insight): The pursuit of wisdom and understanding. In real estate, it seeks to uncover the ideas, ethics, and human truths that shape markets and meaning.

Polity (Governance and Order): The system through which societies regulate property and space. It joins political philosophy with urban policy to explore fairness and structure in land use.

Sociology (Culture and Community): The study of how social behavior influences and is influenced by real estate. It connects trends like gentrification, density, and cohesion to human values.

Space (Design and Experience): More than physical dimension, space reflects how people move, interact, and find purpose within environments.

Stewardship (Care and Continuity): The ethical responsibility to manage property for the benefit of people, community, and the planet.

Sustainability (Balance and Longevity): Designing and maintaining property that meets present needs without limiting future generations. Philosophically, it aligns profit with preservation.

Technology (Transformation and Progress): The innovations reshaping how we build, live, and connect. It raises questions about automation, efficiency, and the human role in the built world.

Topology (Place and Identity): The study of how geography and structure influence personal and communal identity. In real estate, it defines the emotional and spatial relationship between people and their environments.

Value (Worth and Meaning): A measure that goes beyond price, blending financial worth, human experience, and philosophical significance.

Worth (Recognition and Purpose): The acknowledgment of a property's importance not only in economic terms but also in emotional, social, and cultural value.

READERS NOTES

Bonus Section: Case Studies and Reflections

Throughout this book, we've delved into the philosophy of real estate, uncovering how concepts like value, identity, and connection shape the spaces we inhabit. Now, let's ground those ideas in reality by exploring more detailed real-world case studies. These stories illustrate how philosophical principles play out in tangible ways, weaving together residential and commercial real estate while reinforcing the deeper lessons we've explored so far.

Imagine a young couple searching for their first home.

They're drawn to a quiet suburban neighborhood known for its close-knit community and excellent schools. The homes are spacious, with gardens where children can play, and the neighborhood radiates a sense of security and belonging. However, their budget also allows them to consider a sleek, modern apartment in the city center. This urban option offers convenience, proximity to work, and vibrant nightlife, a lifestyle that aligns with their professional ambitions and love for cultural experiences.

Their decision isn't just about practicality, it reflects deeper philosophical questions about identity, belonging, and purpose. The suburban home aligns with the themes of stability and connection explored in *Spatial Identity, Place, and Self*. It speaks to their desire for community and long-term family goals. On the other hand, the city apartment embodies aspirations of vibrancy and individualism, reflecting a different kind of identity tied to ambition and modern living. Ultimately, their choice will reveal how deeply personal values influence real estate decisions, shaping not just where we live but how we live.

In the commercial realm, consider a small business owner deciding where to expand their growing retail brand.

They operate a popular boutique selling locally sourced products, and their current location has become too small to meet growing demand. One option is to lease a storefront in a bustling shopping center. This would give them steady foot traffic, visibility, and access to a larger customer base. However, it also comes with high rental costs and limited control over the space.

The alternative is to purchase a standalone property in an emerging neighborhood. While this offers autonomy and the potential for long-term investment growth, it also carries risks, the area is still developing, and the initial cost is significantly higher. This case ties into the themes of *Ownership and Rights* and *Market Forces,* highlighting the philosophical tension between short-term stability and long-term opportunity. Their eventual choice will reflect their risk tolerance, growth philosophy, and commitment to community impact, showing how business decisions are often rooted in values beyond profit.

On a global scale, let's examine the story of a coastal town transformed by international investment.

For decades, this town was known for its fishing industry and local charm, with modest homes overlooking the ocean. In recent years, it has attracted buyers from across the globe, drawn by its scenic beauty and affordability. New developments have sprung up, luxury condos, upscale resorts, and retail spaces catering to a wealthier clientele.

While this influx of foreign capital boosts property values and local revenue, it also raises concerns about equity and accessibility for longtime residents. Many families find themselves priced out of neighborhoods they've lived in for generations, and the cultural fabric of the town begins to shift. This scenario ties into *Globality* and *Governance,* reflecting on how interconnected markets create both opportunities and challenges. The evolution of this town mirrors the global real estate market's dual role as a driver of progress and a source of tension.

Each of these case studies, residential, commercial, and global, offers a lens through which to view the philosophical principles of real estate.

They show how the spaces we inhabit are shaped by decisions that blend practicality with deeper ideals. Whether it's the personal meaning of a home, the strategic vision of a business, or the societal impact of global markets, real estate is ultimately about people and the values they bring to the spaces they create.

As we reflect on these examples, the suburban couple's dilemma echoes themes from *Emotional Connection to Real Estate,* exploring how feelings of pride, nostalgia, and belonging influence decisions. The business owner's choice connects to *Transformative Impacts,* where innovation and calculated risk define success. And the coastal town's evolution brings us back to *Environmental Considerations,* reminding us of the need to balance progress with responsibility to communities and the environment.

These case studies bring the philosophical principles explored throughout this book to life, grounding abstract ideas in the realities of residential and commercial real estate. They remind us that real estate is not just about property, it's about people, connections, and the ever-evolving spaces that shape our lives.

Consider how these reflections apply to your own experiences.

The decisions you make, whether personal or professional, are part of a larger narrative that connects philosophy with practicality. Let these stories inspire you to see real estate not just as a market but as a profound expression of humanity.

READERS NOTES

Updated List of Books to Date

Willem Tait is the author of several impactful real estate books that examine the dynamic and ever-changing nature of the real estate market. Each book provides valuable strategies, practical insights, and a comprehensive understanding of the key factors influencing the industry. Below is the full list of his published works to date:

Real Estate Law Essentials:
Navigate Cross-Sections, Avoid Pitfalls, and Seize Opportunities. A comprehensive guide to understanding the legal frameworks surrounding real estate, offering practical advice for navigating transactions and mitigating risks.

Proven Principles of Residential Real Estate Investment:
Strategies and Tasks for Building Generational Wealth. A detailed exploration of residential real estate investment strategies, designed to help readers achieve long-term financial security and success.

Practical Principles of Commercial Real Estate Investment:
Tasks and Strategies for Real Estate Success. Focused on commercial real estate, this book provides actionable principles and strategies for navigating the complexities of the market and achieving professional growth.

Real Estate Economics: Property Market Principles and Practices.
This book offers an informative, in-depth analysis of real estate markets, their practices and their underlying principles, and the economic forces driving them.

Raising Money for Real Estate Investment:
Close Deals, Raise Money, Build Wealth. A practical guide to securing funding for real estate projects, this book emphasizes effective deal-making and wealth-building strategies.

Capital Markets and Real Estate:
Bridging Markets for a Global Future. This work explores the intersection of real estate and capital markets, highlighting their convergence and the opportunities that globalization presents for industry professionals.

Real Estate Development and Deal Making:
The Essential Guide for Property Developers, Entrepreneurs, and Dealmakers. This comprehensive guide ties together the foundational principles of property development with innovative strategies for deal-making and entrepreneurship, providing actionable insights for success in the industry.

Psychology of Residential and Commercial Real Estate:
Master the Psychology Behind Real Estate Success. A practical guide into real estate decision making. By uncovering the emotions, motivations, and cognitive biases behind property decisions, this book provides actionable strategies for property success.

Philosophy of Residential and Commercial Real Estate:
Exploring the Intersection of Philosophy, People, Property, Purpose and Spaces. A thoughtful exploration of the deeper meaning behind property and spaces. By examining the beliefs, values, and purposes that shape real estate, this book provides insightful principles for aligning property decisions with vision and intent.

Real Estate Mastery Books

These books are part of the Real Estate Mastery Books, a series designed to equip readers with the tools and knowledge necessary to excel in the fields of real estate and capital markets. This ever-expanding series reflects Willem Tait's commitment to providing actionable insights and strategies. Keep an eye out for upcoming titles in this growing collection, as there are always more exciting additions to come.

Acknowledgement

Writing this book has been a journey of learning, reflection, and exploration, and I am deeply grateful to the many individuals who have contributed to its creation.

To all the coaches, mentors, psychologists, and medical professionals who crossed my path and generously shared their time, wisdom, and expertise, thank you.

Your openness during interviews and your willingness to guide me through your fields of knowledge have been invaluable.

To the property professionals who are deeply passionate about spaces and the people who inhabit them, your insights and experiences have shaped the essence of this book.

From landlords to architects, town planners, property managers, and tenants, your perspectives offered a unique glimpse into the profound connections between property, people, purpose and spaces.

This book is as much a product of these collective contributions as it is of my own reflections.

I am forever indebted to your generosity, dedication, and passion for making spaces more meaningful for the people who live and work in them.

Social Profiles

Willem Tait is committed to staying connected and engaging with his readers. He is active on LinkedIn and X (formerly Twitter), where he shares updates on his latest projects, insights, and resources. Willem is also available for face-to-face consultations, public speaking, and group training sessions through platforms like WhatsApp, Zoom, Google Meet, and Microsoft Teams.

Feel free to reach out on any of these platforms to connect, share ideas, or discuss opportunities for learning and growth. Let's keep building together!

Email: willemtait@outlook.com

Email: willemtait@gmail.com

Amazon Author:

https://www.amazon.com/author/willemtait

Goodreads: https://www.goodreads.com/willemtait

Linktree: https://linktr.ee/willemtait

Calendly https://calendly.com/willemtait

Linkedin: https://www.linkedin.com/in/willemtait

X: https://x.com/willemtait

Reddit: https://www.reddit.com/user/WillemTait/

Blogger: https://willemtaitauthor.blogspot.com/

Substack: https://willemtait.substack.com/

Medium: https://willemtaitblog.medium.com/

Pinterest: https://.pinterest.com/willemtait/

Mentorship, Coaching, Consulting and Public Speaking

As a dedicated professional with a passion for real estate, business, law, and economics, I thrive on sharing actionable insights and practical strategies that empower individuals and teams to achieve their goals.

My expertise spans real estate investment, business consulting, personal growth, and the intricate connections between legal and economic frameworks, allowing me to offer a well-rounded perspective tailored to diverse challenges and ambitions.

Through public speaking engagements, customised mentorship programs, and dynamic one-on-one or group coaching sessions, I aim to inspire, educate, and guide.

Whether addressing an audience of hundreds or working closely with a small team, my mission is to deliver value-driven insights that leave a lasting impact.

If you're seeking a keynote speaker to energise and inform your event, a consultant to elevate your business strategies, or a mentor to foster personal and professional growth, I'm here to collaborate. My approach integrates years of hands-on experience with a solid foundation in real estate, law and economics, ensuring the strategies I share are both practical and informed by robust principles.

Let's connect to explore how I can help you or your organisation unlock new opportunities and achieve meaningful success.

Together, we can create strategies that inspire growth, drive innovation, and deliver measurable results.

LinkedIn: https://www.linkedin.com/in/willemtait/

Mail: willemtait@outlook.com

Author Bio

Willem Tait is an accomplished author, real estate expert, and industry mentor whose journey through the worlds of property investment, real estate development, capital markets, and human understanding has inspired professionals across the globe.

With decades of experience, Willem has become a trusted voice in real estate strategy, capital markets integration, and the transformative power of mentorship, all underpinned by a deep interest in psychology, philosophy, and the profound connections between people and spaces.

Willem's passion for education, critical thinking, and professional growth is reflected in the nine insightful books authored to date.

Each work delves into the intricate dynamics of real estate while exploring the psychological and philosophical forces that shape decision-making and human interaction.

Offering practical strategies, actionable insights, and thought-provoking perspectives, Willem's writings span topics from sustainability and innovation to navigating complex financial landscapes.

This prolific body of work solidifies his position as an authority in the field, bridging the gap between theory, practice, and the human experience with clarity and expertise.

Beyond writing, Willem Tait holds a strong academic foundation, having pursued advanced studies that inform a nuanced understanding of real estate, economics, psychology, and philosophy.

This dedication to lifelong learning complements a hands-on approach to mentoring aspiring professionals, helping them achieve their goals in real estate and beyond.

Known for his ability to break down complex concepts into accessible knowledge, Willem empowers readers and mentees alike to navigate the evolving challenges of the industry while fostering a deeper understanding of the motivations and principles that drive success.

Whether guiding readers through the intricacies of capital markets, exploring the philosophical meaning of spaces, or inspiring the next generation of leaders,

Willem Tait continues to shape the conversation around real estate and its future.

This blend of expertise, passion, and a commitment to human connection ensures that Willem remains not just a specialist, but a trailblazer in the ever-changing world of real estate, capital markets, and the broader human narrative.

Upcoming Projects

Thank you for joining me on this journey into the fascinating world of real estate. This book is just the first step in what I hope will be a long and meaningful exploration of the strategies, insights, and opportunities that define the real estate landscape.

I'm excited to share that my next book is already well underway. It builds upon the foundation laid here, diving deeper into the the future of real estate and what we call in industry PropTech. Backed by even more in-depth research and practical case studies, this upcoming work will provide actionable advice and fresh perspectives designed to empower your success in this ever-evolving field.

We Value Your Feedback!

Thank you for taking the time to read this book. Your insights and experiences mean the world to me, and I would love to hear your thoughts.

If you found the strategies and principles in this book helpful, please consider leaving a review on Amazon or your preferred platform. Your feedback not only helps me improve but also helps other readers discover valuable resources for their commercial real estate journey.

Sharing your thoughts can inspire others to take the next step in their investment journey. Whether it's a quick rating or a detailed review, your voice makes a difference!

Thank you again for your time and trust in this book. Wishing you success in all your real estate ventures!

READERS NOTES

READERS NOTES

READERS NOTES

READERS NOTES

Portfolio of Books by Willem Tait

For more, kindly see www.amazon.com/author/willemtait

BUSINESS BOOKS

1. **Real Estate Law Essentials:** Navigate Cross-Sections, Avoid Pitfalls, and Seize Opportunities.
2. **Proven Principles of Residential Real Estate Investment:** Strategies and Tasks for Building Generational Wealth.
3. **Practical Principles of Commercial Real Estate Investment:** Tasks and Strategies for Real Estate Success.
4. **Real Estate Economics:** Property Market Principles and Practices.
5. **Raising Money for Real Estate Investment:** Close Deals, Raise Money, Build Wealth.
6. **Capital Markets and Real Estate:** How Money and Capital Shapes the Property Market.
7. **Real Estate Development and Deal Making:** The Essential Guide for Property Developers, Entrepreneurs, and Dealmakers.
8. **Psychology of Residential and Commercial Real Estate:** Master the Psychology Behind Real Estate Success.
9. **Philosophy of Residential and Commercial Real Estate:** Exploring the Intersection of Philosophy, People, Property, Purpose and Spaces.
10. **Economics of Banking and Money:** Insight into Power, Trust, and Change.
11. **The Future of Real Estate:** PropTech, Sustainability and Design

SELF-HELP AND MOTIVATIONAL BOOKS

1. **Sort Your Crap Out:** Own Your Choices, Silence Your Critic. Get Stuff Done
2. **Dammit, Get It Together:** Stop Making Excuses and Start Living the Life You Deserve
3. **Stop Giving a Damn and Start Living:** Cut the Crap. Focus on What Matters. Live Fully
4. **Dammit, It's Your Life:** Own Your Mind, Time, and Choices
5. **Dammit, Stop Being Overwhelmed and Overworked:** Reclaim Your Time, Energy, and Sanity

ANNOTATED AND COMMENTARY

1. **The Way to Wealth** (Annotated): With Motivational Commentary by Willem Tait
2. **The Art Of War:** (Annotated): Proven Modern Strategies for Winning in Business, Leadership, and Life by Willem Tait

www.ingramcontent.com/pod-product-compliance
Lightning Source LLC
Chambersburg PA
CBHW071549220526
45469CB00003B/954